MANNIVERSARY

The Roots Of a Man

Michael Evans

MANNIVERSARY: The Roots of A Man

ISBN: 979-8-218-19830-5

Book cover design and interior layout provided by Self Publish Me, LLC Publishing Consulting and Book Design Services for Independent Authors.
www.selfpublishme.com | email:
info@selfpublishme.com

This book is dedicated to
Rechelle Evans.

Contents

Contents

Introduction

The tree is symbolic because the ROOTS OF A MAN is necessary to give life to all communities and families. Manniversary is a celebration of change where a man understands his name and the importance of leading and serving by example, where God is head over his life. The sole purpose of this book is to TEACH the importance of recognizing and honoring God as the head of your home. It would help one understand how much we get in our way. We often complain about others and their differences instead of focusing on the person in front of the mirror. Some of us create an intolerable relationship with ourselves because we do not have standards or a foundation built on commitment, compassion, and consistency. Because of this, we sometimes require anyone who comes into our circumference to possess these traits. Hypocrisy was my foundation, but my foundation changed as I got to know God, Jesus, and the Holy Spirit. It's simple. Anyone can change. You just have to get rid of the titles and put in the work. Once you become great at listening, then you can lead. You can even build a fiduciary relationship based on God, love, and sacrifice. Now, this is the foundation of my life...enjoy.

Chapter 1
In the Beginning

B eing born under the astrological sign of Libra taught me how to weigh my scales and create balance in my life. My life first began in Chicago, IL., at Mercy Hospital. Significantly, I acknowledge both of my parents regardless of my life experiences. There was a platform but no plan, which greatly impacted who I am and why I move the way I do. We resided on the south side of Chicago, more specifically, Englewood. There were a lot of Black homeowners, and the neighborhood was peaceful the majority of the time. What I remember most is that my mother always tried to keep the house together, and my father never fully immersed himself in his role as the head of the household.

My brothers and I got disciplined together even when only one of us made a mistake. In my mind, this was unfair, but this way of living helped me understand why it was important not to surround myself with wrongdoing. My father was a great example of this. He would get paid on Friday and would be broke by Monday. This trend was his normal behavior. Although my father had many skills, he never taught me and my brothers anything. Because of this, I felt I did not know anything and often found myself on a quest to find my purpose. My place to see inspiration was outside. It was where my imagination would take over, and I believed I was invincible. My siblings and I would always have the time of our lives! We would climb on top of houses, in trees, and on top of garages. We also played sports and childhood games. My favorite game to play was Catch a Girl, Kiss a Girl.

My behavior in school was fantastic, and I am proud to say that I never failed any subject. I loved this considering the progress that some of my brothers made. My three brothers and I were all trying to define and find ourselves growing up.

My oldest brother always stayed in trouble. He was deemed "Mr. Can't Do Right." He was the reason that we got disciplined 90% of the time. We weren't the only ones that needed discipline. I believe my father could have used a lesson in restraint himself. Instead of spending money on his family, he enjoyed gambling on horses, liquor, and weed. My father was stubborn and never listened to anyone but himself. Because of this, I did not know what a man was.

I can recall times when he would come in drunk and high, and I could hear my mother asking him why he was in that condition. I loved my father and believed he could do no wrong. He would argue with my mother sometimes, and I vividly remember when he put his hands on her! At that time, we were too little to protect her, and I promised myself that I would never physically abuse my significant other. I desperately wanted my father to be a father, and while he tried, it wasn't good enough at times. I wanted him to teach me life lessons, discuss the needed information, and go on trips with me. The only trip that my father took us on was to the horse races. We would spend countless hours in the elements seeing him lose our future, and he would not stop until he lost it all! I remember meeting my Uncle Charlie, my father's brother from California. He was an excellent young man that was trying to find his purpose. When he got grounded, he sought refuge in the Lord. He lived with us, and we had some of the best times with our uncle. Uncle Charlie introduced my brothers and me to a show called Samurai Sunday. When it came on, we would have an all-out karate fight, including my uncle. Lol! These are memories that I will never forget.

I loved going to church with Uncle Charlie on Sunday. He attended Second Mount Vernon church in Chicago, IL. It was a blessing because the people there treated you like their own. It was nice to meet new people and see active fathers. We would eat at McDonald's, across the street from the church. It seemed like everything would be okay for those moments, but the devil always has a way of trying to break up something good. I remember when my uncle had a mental breakdown. It was traumatizing to witness, and as time progressed, we eventually learned that my uncle had sickle cell. Until then, we had no clue what it was, but we soon discovered how deadly it could be. When my uncle passed, things drastically changed in the household. My father, who was already selfish, became even more selfish, and my mother got to the point where she stopped caring about their relationship. My mother is a great woman and was the backbone of the family. She always stayed true even when things were rough in her marriage.

I remember when I was one year old and lived with my Aunt Olivia, who loved me unconditionally. She always read to me and reminded me why serving God and being obedient was necessary. She always dressed me in nice clothes when we went to church. She ensured I ate and was put to bed at a specific time. Her routine taught me structure; she went home to heaven when I turned three. I never knew my grandmother, but the women in my family are all great.

My mother is a God-fearing woman. She never struggled with her faith, as far as I knew. She always ensured she went to work to provide for the family even though my father was there and chose not to do so. We went to church at The New Testament F.B.C. on the south side of Chicago, where Dr. Trudie Trimm was pastor. Dr. Trimm was notable because men were mainly called to preach during that time. Christ has always influenced me, but I needed to understand who Jesus was and wanted to know more.

My mother always found time to ensure we were okay. I took pride in my grades and behaved well. I understood how hard my mother had to work. The frustration on her face from her job alone showed that my mother felt unappreciated. On the other hand, my father and his lack of appreciation is another story. My mother would always make sure we had shoes and clothes before she did something for herself. Her God sister, my other mother, Mama Ann, has always blessed our family. Whatever my mother needed, she was always willing to assist, no questions asked.

I have seen what friendship, family, and commitment genuinely mean through these times. The standards make sense, but there were still some things that I needed to understand. The arguments that my parents had were all brought on by my father. He seemed jealous of my mother because of his insecurities. I once wanted to run away because I believed there was something better in the world. Thank God that never happened. Back then, I didn't understand. I thought everything was great, but the truth is that we, as a family, were broken. We had a lot of roaches and a lot of mice, and this was due to my father not caring about the house he lived in. I don't recall ever seeing him clean up or even own a lawnmower.

At age 10, I wanted to ask my father

questions, but he was never around to answer them. I wanted to be a part of someone else's family because when I asked my best friend Willie's father a question, he would give me the answer. The different feelings inside my head would create anger inside my heart, which caused me to resent my father. The incident that further plagued this resentment was when we lost our home. Life made no sense to me because my father had the money to pay the bills. He made enough money to have paid the house off in two years. That was one of the lowest points in my childhood, so I promised myself that I would never lose a home due to my ignorance.

My grandmother figure in my life was Ms. Lee Bell God rest her soul because she was a beautiful woman who treated my mother like her daughter. Whatever my mother needed, she gave it to her no matter what. It's crazy that my father didn't even have a sense of dignity when we moved back into the studio apartment where Ms. Lee Bell resided. It broke my heart when my brother stole from Ms. Lee Bell. That day my father was mad at him, but I was angry at my father because he stole our dreams. Through the grace of God, we got an apartment, and my mother put it in her name. The owner, who went by the name "Little Sister," allowed us to move in. I never really got to thank Ms. Lee Bell for allowing us somewhere to lay our heads. My mother thanked her and was heartbroken about what had transpired during our stay. My father was on drugs, and things worsened when we moved out of Ms. Lee Bell's studio.

Chapter 2
Spiraling Out of Control

J ust like any other person who can hear and see, exposure to what you are hearing and seeing sometimes puts you in a place where you become a product of your environment, whether it may be harmful or positive. These things become significant in your life and can cause your path to becoming inconsistent and spiral out of control. From the age of 1 to 3 years old, you emulate the things you see around you, and based on your mother's pregnancy, your emotional status coming into the world can be up or down. I wanted to determine the impact on a child's emotional stability if the father or significant other was at home during the pregnancy. I started observing my grandchildren and other parents of children whom I consider family. Would it make the mother feel valued? Would the child come out with less emotional distress? My findings were accurate. If there was no one other than the mother at home, and she had to struggle physically and mentally, the child's emotional distress level was very high. These vital components play a role in who one ultimately becomes because anything that doesn't have guidance grows wild. Therefore, this can influence the negative downfall of a life journey and cause the child not to trust the process or believe in their dreams. It is essential that those that choose to have children realize the importance of planting seeds in fertile soil. When the soil is fertile, your child has a greater chance of manifesting success in their life.

My Aunt Olvia encouraged me to dream as a child. I remember her saying, "You will be great one day and live a life of abundance for God." She often prayed over me, setting a field of faith around me. When she passed away, it felt like the dreams also left my spirit. I returned home and saw my mother was pregnant and about to bring another child into the fold. That experience made me feel like failure was my norm. However, my mother showed us what faith was through trying times. She focused on staying motivated with four boys and my father because she was the glue in the family, and without her, we would fail. We were all developing the traits in our DNA, both good and bad.

I have always had a love for music. I loved when my father would blast his stereo every Friday, but he would drink and smoke, also. His actions became the norm in my mind. On Saturday, I enjoyed watching cartoons and college football and playing outside. My dreams started to become more evident as I grew. We would imitate our favorite athlete in each game we played at that time. My favorite show was The Cosby Show. I wished my dad would watch it to see the display of the three C's: communication, compassion, and commitment. To me, those were the things that made a man. I wanted to become all those things. I could see it each time I closed my eyes, playing football for the Chicago Bears and baseball for the Chicago Cubs.

I imagined coming home to my intelligent wife and always telling her about the adversity of my day. I envisioned attending church on Sunday and becoming part of the ministry one day. After coming home from a long day's work, I dreamed I would look for my children to ensure that I hugged them and discussed their day with them. I would be getting ready for what my wife prepared for dinner as I helped the children with their homework before we sat down as a family. After dinner, I would make sure they took a bath. I would pray with them before I tucked them in for bed. The following day before I went to practice, I would get up and say good morning to my kids and wife to make sure they were in good spirits and leave for work. Unfortunately, all of this was just a part of my imagination. Reality took over once I opened my eyes to find my three brothers and me in this small room with roaches crawling around and mice singing in the walls.

We had one bathroom, which had a tub and no shower. I often took bird baths because we had to get in and out in time to get to breakfast at school. Otherwise, we had to wait for lunch, which felt like forever. We did not have food at home, so we depended on eating at school. Sometimes I could practice my dreams occasionally as we played sports outside with my friends and Uncle Joe, who lived with us briefly. He taught us different things about his upbringing, like fighting, baseball, and cooking. I still lacked the understanding of what a man was through this timeframe, so my television father became my dad. I would try understanding girls so I could find my wife at an early age, but being vertically challenged meant that most of my choices were taller than me, making me less confident. Subsequently, my focus was on sports. My Uncle Charlie enrolled us in baseball, and I was ready to become great and looking forward to doing so. I had an OK season, but this experience would not last long because my uncle became ill and passed away. I was back at square one again, looking around for someone to help me get to the next level, so I could make my dreams come true. It felt like darkness.

I was looking around at this time and saw the older guys driving nice cars and some of my friend's older brothers doing strange things for money. Even though this looked interesting, I knew this wasn't wise because they always dispersed when the police came around. It still made me want to rethink my dream, but I stayed focused on the task by practicing football. I was fast, quick on cutbacks, and skinny and solid so that I could take a hit. As I grew older, we had more problems in the house, and the neighborhood started to change. The older guys started gang recruitment, and there were more breaks in an already broken community.

The drug of choice was crack, so many kids' parents did whatever they could to get high. Around this time, we were influenced by guns, sex, food stamps, and cash. I played around but wouldn't commit because my dream still felt possible. My father lost his mind and started playing with money, and the next thing I knew, we lost our home. Thank God I graduated out of eighth grade before we were evicted. It meant I didn't have to defend my father's character with my peers constantly. My dream was shifting then, and I could feel it starting to change when we moved to a new area where the gangs and people were different. However, we all wanted the same thing—respect.

Going to church on the southeast side and living there were two different things because you never knew what was on the other side of Cottage Grove. Cottage Grove was a street that divided the rival gangs. Through God's grace, my family could find a place where my mother could work while we attended school. I attended Martin Luther King High School, which was an honor knowing what he stood for, and I eventually received a diploma with his name on it.

At that time, my dreams shifted due to new friends and my old acquaintance – violence. I had always thought out things before I did them, and some would say they were premeditated, but I had to be this way due to false leadership, bullies, and fake friends. Even though I did it reluctantly, those things kept me three steps ahead of everyone. As friends became foes due to the separation of gangs, my dreams changed again. The neighborhood we lived in became a war zone. Some days I was unsure if I would live to see another day. When I closed my eyes, I dreamed of having a child who could carry on my name. I never wanted anything I did to affect my mother negatively, so I did not fight some battles. My missions were out of sight from the locals, which kept karma off my back. I was introduced to all walks of deception in the devil's playground and learned much about the love of money. Sports became second to my sex goal, inspired by my Uncle Joe, who told me, "A woman has heard all types of conversation." He told me, "It's not what you say; it's how you say it." This substandard advice led me to perfect my sex talk. It granted me access to lots of panty parties.

Schoolwork was a breeze because I caught on quickly and understood how to fly below the radar. I was so excited the first time I had sex that it only lasted thirty seconds. I even lied to the older girl about it not being my first time.

I used my favorite tool, music, to assist in this process the second time. At that time in my life, I loved juke music. If I played it, she got the business, and if she talked crazy before I hit it, she got the DJ Deon mix, and I would get it in for 30 minutes. I disrespected my mother while she was at work and treated my bedroom like a gynecologist's office. The sad part is that anything done without a plan has consequences, and I was grateful for the free clinics at that time. Confident young ladies wanted me, and it was my first time, but not my last time being polyamorous. It also was my first time having sex on the lakefront. I had them all to myself and was ready to get them all. I was so excited I started on the first one as the others watched. It took a lot of force because she was a virgin; however, how she talked made me think otherwise. I was more into it than I anticipated while the others watched. I never got to the other three. They were mad, and I never got a chance to have sex with them due to their friend catching feelings for me.

At that point, my penis ran my life, and the main focus was vagina counts. My associates and I were going to the museum on 55th Street, where I was introduced to all shades of girls and women. I felt like a fat kid in a cake store and ensured I got at least 5 to 10 numbers since my odds of smashing were 2 out of 10. The best part was that they lived all over. It would give me a sense of fearlessness as time progressed, and I had a chance to meet new people I would encounter later in life. I vowed that wherever she was, I was going to get it. I sometimes found myself in rough spots, but I accomplished the mission 90% of the time. I lost The other 10% due to haters. I also experienced this hatred in my hood, making me go harder.

The neighborhood haters hustled and paid for sex, and I smashed for free. I soon realized that time was money. I could have been practicing my childhood dreams in the gym or the weight room, but her smell, smile, shape, and feel were intriguing. The sad part is that my dream of finding her was lost because I knew nothing of a heart or sound mind. I only knew about ass and titties. My first encounter with one whom I wanted to make my wife would be short-lived due to my ego and pride, so I moved on and found another loyal one. She didn't like school much, so it was a turnoff, but I still tried to trust the process. Now, I still had multiple girls I dealt with, but I was trying to slow down, and the truth was that each one had a piece of what I thought the other one I should be with needed. We broke up but never lost contact, so I moved on again. This next one was special, but she was slicker than a can of oil. We met through a mishap. My brother was dating her friend, and she came over with a pretty smile and attitude in all the right places. At first, she couldn't stand my guts, but eventually, I won her over. It's crazy how circumstances made us connect at that time.

Through those crazy four years of high school, I could have made 10% of Chicago pregnant, but only one girl carried my seed then. When boys behave like dogs, we never get to know the girl or anything significant about them, and we wonder why we go through what we do. I discovered her age and personal information, but it didn't matter because I had what I had asked for. I had someone to carry my name. I graduated from high school, and she sat there as I crossed the stage with no plans. I was just going with the flow and hoping I could rely on my instincts to provide for my family. Seeing death and being a part of violence is not what I wanted for my son. I was searching for an understanding, but I decided to fake it until I could make it.

We proceeded to go to her home, building 4555, after graduation. It was my first time going there, and as always, I could feel the hate from her ex-boyfriends. It was nothing new, but I was happy to have finished high school. Reflecting on that time, I remember telling her I wasn't coming over until after graduation due to the gang affiliation in certain areas. Through all of this, my son was born, but a dog is going to be a dog, and I wasn't there when she needed me. I knew I would have to suffer the consequences of my absence sooner or later. At that time, I moved in with my associate's grandmother and family, Sarah. Sarah was a great woman whom I loved as my other mother. I enjoyed having conversations with her about life and her past. She was a beautiful person inside and out, and she taught me a lot through our conversations over the years. I tried college for one semester, and while it was OK, I needed money.

My second child was on the way with a different young lady then. I found myself in the same scenario with a different narrative. It was crazy because I had never told my son's mother that I was having another child, and I soon learned that what is done in the dark will come to light. My associates and I took a trip looking for jobs and came to what I called the promised land. We did not know what a father was or what being a real man consisted of, but now the journey began. The worst thing I ever put in the atmosphere was that I would never be like my father. While this is what I desired, I didn't have a plan that would prevent me from being the same person in a different place. My new dream was to run a successful hustle business in which I was to learn the supplier's language to recoup the negative and turn it into something positive. I viewed all the situations I have been in, and I knew that the way I saw it, things had to change due to new surroundings. For me to be successful, I had to embrace the change.

There is racism in all divisions of life. You must learn how to take the good out of the bad. When you first received the vision, it was a thought in which you understood change had to happen for it to become a reality. Depending on your chosen route, it will take longer if there is no system or foundation you have to build. The most important part of the equation is the company you keep around you. I learned a lesson from the deaths of good brothers on the street. Most of the time, their deaths were caused by the people with whom they were affiliated. That is why the phrase, "You are the company you keep," is so accurate. I believed my son and daughter were my focus, so I concentrated on improving their lives.

I needed to change what I saw, and just like that, everything opened up in a place I had never seen before in the suburbs of Illinois. I soon began communicating with different walks of life and moved forward at my job. Once doors started to open, I desired to purchase a McDonald's. However, just like anything negative in life, there is a price to pay, and I almost paid with my life due to karma. You reap what you sow, point blank. I made a move without thinking, and I found myself trading places at a time when things were looking up. Remember what I said about the dark coming to light?

While I was in intensive care, my daughter's mother came to visit, my son's mother was by my side, and the heart monitor started racing faster due to me never telling my son's mother I had a daughter. It broke her heart that moment, creating a second wedge between us. Because I was the hoe that I was, another woman came to visit once they took the tubes out and moved me to a room. We had sex in the hospital. Women always came through and would listen to my problems as I would theirs. I became involved in situations I should not have been in and cared about fake friends. I always tried to help those around me out of a jam.

Kicking it would cost me millions. I have always had two people inside me, and we always would have conversations based on the decision to react or respond.

Reacting to a situation causes consequences due to the temperament of your actions, making you move without understanding. It always costs you something, especially in the streets. When you respond, you should utilize the 9-second rule of counting down to calm down and visualize what can take place and what you can lose. It gives you an understanding of why you should choose freedom/life over making a point. The outcome is always a lesson learned; you are still in the flesh. We plan differently when the road once traveled only creates detours. I was still searching for my purpose, and the mall where I worked turned into a high school again. If you listen to those streets, they always tell you the truth, and I remember when they said no one could see the greatness in you until you see it in you.

Simply put, I invest in myself first and add those who want the same around me. This way, we move with understanding and not force.

The world is a business; if you allow the process to happen, you begin to see people and places for what they are and how significant they are in your life. I learned this later in life, so let's get on track. My taste for women of different nationalities made me start a new list in which I had a goal to understand the vagina due to watching porn and seeing the different orgasms of other women. If you notice, I had the energy to become successful, but I focused on the wrong things. Working at McDonald's introduced me to all walks of life, many different benefits, and access to so much information that college would have never taught me. I learned that experience is the best teacher, and I wanted to know the good and the bad. This type of journey comes with sacrifice for something or someone. Unfortunately, it was my children. I was exactly like my father during this time. However, I buy my kids things; I am not around them due to ignorance. I forgot my dream, and another generation is going through the same thing again because of a lack of leadership and spirituality. I was still out there, and even worse, I was messing around where I ate, and you know what kind of problems this can cause, especially when you are hitting on others in the mall.

I should have been an acrobat because I was flipping situations around with these women. I learned from the past to be upfront, although they felt it was different because we had an agreement. I started giving relationship advice to this beautiful dark-skinned lady who looked and was shaped like a chocolate Barbie doll. The advice worked for me being the hypocrite I was at the time. I was giving good advice, but I needed to follow my instructions. The dog in me had a hidden agenda, but the gentlemen in me considered her a friend. Amidst this, I got a transfer, and it started to mess with my money. Although it was a positive money boost, it changed my time for my personal life change because it required more job commitment. Due to this, I had to put the sex list to the side. I completed 70% of the list but became bored with no real relationship. My business life started to slip due to me shifting and seeing the actual world for what it was, and I was given a choice. Eventually, I lost everything except my soul. Through my reset, I ran into the single chocolate Barbie doll. I had messed up some of my relationships with other women. We became each other's release station, mentally and physically. Our relationship became a connection in which we would talk about anything. Things in my life changed, and I found myself back on top. Everything was legit.

My new choice of women was now

independent, but I would soon fall for one young lady who needed to fit the qualifications.

I decided that I wanted to get to know her. I took this journey and found myself in yet another situation. I would do things to her, like lick her downstairs labia. From there, I told myself it was just going to be her, and I was ready to commit until I forgot she was three years younger and didn't understand where my heart and mind had been. She did the unthinkable and offered me a menajahtwa. Any other time I would have, but I wanted something different, which started me back to my hoe-ish ways. My relationship with her was over mentally, but her mother became my other mother, and she will always be another vital part of my life going forward.

I started being at the bachelor pad more often and smashing more women. Then, I ran into the one who got away when I was younger. Sadly, I wasn't ready for her, but I was willing to try, and I thank her for being so influential in my life in so many ways.

Although I did not know what love was at the time, the first time we felt each other, it was like a movie scene where she wanted to say no, but her soul said yes. We kissed as the rain started to fall, as did her clothes in the front seat of the Lumina, and with each stroke, her climax was wetter and wetter. It was one of those nights when nature took over and won. She was the one I wanted to give in to, although I was still a hoe. I stopped for a while, and I remember my fake friend saying that I was pussy whipped, and I remember reacting and saying I wasn't. I returned to my old ways while disregarding my heart and mind saying she was the one. I lost her, only to discover that my fake friends were snitching and telling her false information based on what I told them about my actions in the bachelor pad. It was crazy how she would pop up after someone had just left. I learned a valuable lesson, so I never showed them how I got money then. I saw the signs, but I disregarded them, and I have no regrets in life. Now, I am back on the list, and I have completed only 90% of it and learned that I missed a lot of investments and time with my children because I was doing me. I hooked up with my old girlfriend one day, only for her to become pregnant, and I was unsure if it was my daughter. I later found out that she was my child. At the time, my son's mother and I were not friends because I kept seeing myself going in circles, but we were trying to make it work this time. I moved in, which was great because I got to know my mother-in-law and spent time with my son. As always, my ignorance would cause us to break up again, and I went back to becoming a doorknob where everyone gets a turn. I found myself now having sex with older women, mothers, daughters, sisters, and also friends. Damn, as I look back, I realize that I had loyalty to no one. At the time, I was a porn star. Give me some weed, a fifth of Remy Martin, and turn on R. Kelly, and I was taking on all five at once with no problem. I was knocking them out because I felt it was my duty when they called. I had a lot of mercy fucks as well because I thought all women needed some dick at the time. Yes, I was a confused individual searching for my soul in women by having sex with whoever would allow me to do so. It impacted how I felt about myself. Having unprotected sex can lead to STDs and pregnancies that are not wanted. You find yourself trying to figure out if these fuck buddies are being truthful, but how can they be when we both seek comfort? It creates children and parents who are confused and not ready, and the child loses every time.

My son's mother and I would try again, and she moved in with me this time. Things sometimes felt okay, but I had these urges and found myself hitting on past women and some new ones. What was worse was that I did not have an issue looking her in the face the following day when she came home from work. She had some things going on as well. I remember she had on some night gear once and tried to convince me it was nothing. Silly rabbit tricks are for kids. Regardless of whether it was true, I still had the nerve to be mad despite what I was doing. Eventually, we would hit rock bottom and break up. It was crazy because she still had a key to the house, but we were not together. She started snooping around and found a letter from my lady in Mexico. She got mad and damaged all my shoes and expensive clothing. It was the first time I wanted to inflict harm on my son's mother, and I remember calling her, cursing at her, and threatening her way of life. I eventually reached the police and got a restraining order on her. Just like any cheater, it always hurts when karma comes around. We were not at our best during this time in life, so when I heard that she was pregnant, you already knew my thoughts, especially after what she had done. I lived a misunderstood lifestyle in which I would take and enjoy the comfort of other women's sexuality, new and old. This mental state caused me not to be focused on my children's future due to my selfish ways.

My intention was never to hurt anyone throughout this process, but how can I say that when hurting others and not being truthful to myself? My son was now living with his mother, and where they were wasn't a better situation. I had to push my pride aside and eventually move them back in. I had to try and be more consistent at being a father, and I had to be committed to the relationship. I became a better father but still cheated in my relationship with my son's mother. I would meet good women and enjoy them as friends, but I always started thinking with the wrong head. It caused a lot of anguish for myself and others due to all the hearts attached to my choices. I could not see all this then, but things become evident once you reflect and look back. Sometimes, it felt like we were on our way up, and then we hit rock bottom. It was due to the person leading the relationship.

I wasn't prepared, and the person trying to teach me was a great leader of a different race. I was taught ignorance against caucasian men, so I could not receive his guidance.

When you allow the world into your upbringing, you are blinded by what God is preparing you for, causing you to miss out on opportunities. Time is money. I spent a lot of time on broken thoughts because of improper decision-making. I thought of a way to try and balance things by getting a house with my son's mother and her father. I had been dealing with my issues, and it was considered to be my first investment. I wanted this house for my family. At that time, I was being a hypocrite in my advice. The problem was that I never got rid of my closet, and because I could still access some of the women, I struggled with being truthful. It is hard to be friends after a relationship when "what if" is still possible, and neither of you has provided closure. We started this new life in a new area, but the same old shenanigans would happen. I wanted to get married, but we broke apart not even 18 months in. I found myself entertaining a relationship with a "friend." It was terrible because I did not give myself time to prepare for her and detox from sexual dealings.

My friend and I became a couple, and we were great together. We accepted each other's kids as our own. We talked, dreamed, enjoyed each other, and loved some of the same artists and food. Her shape fit my shape, and we were compatible. Things were going so well that I asked her to marry me, and she said yes. We were planning everything, and then something happened. I've always requested any woman who is a friend not to ask about my son's mother or anything I have done for her. I spent $2000 on my friends' ring then she wanted a car. I told her no because I had just bought her a ring. She commented about my son's mother, and I gave in.

I called the wedding off months later and left her. I went back home, but first, I had to see what my kid's mother wanted to do. At that time, she was with another guy she enjoyed, who came through occasionally. She had to decide to try with me or stay with him. I did not make this decision because who am I to give her an ultimatum? Although she chose me, it would not come without conflict due to the history between her and this particular person. It hurts because you don't like eating what you dish out.

My words said that I wanted the relationship, but my actions differed. We were going through so many different evils in that house. It was crazy, and we faced adversity at the highest level. Things happened around us, to our kids, and within our families. I was dealing with the two people inside me. One who wanted to be committed, and the other who gave two fucks. I found a war going on, and I had to regain control. I was preparing to go on a mission one day because my son's mother's phone had pocket-dialed me. You hear what you want sometimes, and this deters you from being empowered to handle your business. It is crazy when you are not a trustworthy person as well. We, as people, would avoid these situations if we were honest with ourselves at least 90% of the time. I decided to try and do better and eventually asked her to marry me and start a new chapter in our lives. This time I proposed. She said yes, which caused a weight to be lifted off my shoulders. Now, I finally got to become a husband and try to be committed to the relationship.

The issue was letting these other situations go for good. I have learned that you must become a great listener of reason and compassion to understand the "I will" before you say "I do."

Leading up to the wedding, crazy things almost prevented it from happening. First, there was a family fight, then the truth about a situation came out, and last, we started having second thoughts about each other. Thinking back, the only thing that saved this occasion was the fact that it was a family reunion for the both of us and because I spent money on the ceremony. The ceremony was spectacular, and it was one of the best times of my life. The blessing was that my uncles could attend, and my little sister was also at the wedding. God rest their souls. They would all go home to be with the Lord within the following year. We did not have a traditional wedding. We did it our way. My cousin recorded it, but I lost the tape! Thank God I have the wedding book. The next day was the family reunion, and I had to be at the park at 5:00 a.m. In my mind, my new bride would have wanted to lay with me for those four hours, but nope, she wanted to hang out with her sisters. It would start the first day of our marriage off with drama. I sucked it in as usual and kept going. We had both of our families out, and we had a beautiful time. Afterward, I was banking on the honeymoon to be the best time of our lives because we were married now. I was looking for her to want to be held and be more affectionate. However, she was in the same old routine, creating dysfunction within me.

I started to return to my old ways and question my career again. Karma is accurate, and regardless of how you dish it, when it comes back, you will be lost and wondering, Why me?

Before one year passed, I was backsliding and committing the ultimate sin in marriage—cheating. I found myself about to lose everything just to go dipping in the genes on this mission. Being ignorant would ultimately cost me time and money, and I almost lost my name. I think things through to avoid stuff like this, but that one time when you run off impulse will cause you to risk it all. You will start thinking it's better on the other side because this person does this and this or because of their sexual or physical looks.

You might think that person talks or feels

better but believe me, it's not worth it. Stick to what is for sure and understand that it will work if you trust the process and be honest with yourself and your partner. The journey of an uphill and downhill marriage began to kick in. As always, I will say it and not portray it. The thing that I had become accustomed to is being a hypocrite. I would sit there knowing that I always lose when I don't apply what I say to my life.

I can obtain it when I commit to something. It was negative; therefore, it was short-lived due to no positive foundation. I fell. Now, I am getting back up. I lost my identity, and I wanted her to trust me more, follow my decision-making, and be more affectionate regarding lovemaking.

I felt these things should not be an issue; as always, that wasn't the case. The frustrations that I dealt with made me want my woman to embrace me and share a glance and a wet kiss when we were in the same space. When it was time to make love, I would not always want to be the aggressor seeking her affection. I wanted her to show signs of liking me sexually and physically. It was not the case, and I would find myself searching for this when things became overwhelming, whether due to work, the house, or the streets. Now, the women were not oblivious to my situation of being married.

In some cases, they were also going through the same thing with their significant other. We were wrong for what we did, but we both felt wanted and appreciated for that moment. I would be in and out of this situation for quite some time. I wanted my wife to listen to what I asked her, so I could change and become a better man. It always seemed to go in one ear and out the other.

Looking around you and not having the space inside you that feels like you are progressing can make you lash out and search for additional attention and direct energy towards things that don't matter. I knew I should focus on my children and not my personal feelings because they were always in the middle of these life battles. I searched for things I should have had in place before I said, "I do." Now, I wanted out, so I jumped into another relationship. I remember getting what I considered to be the perfect situational relationship. She was extra affectionate, she paid attention to detail, and she was a free spirit. She was everything I thought I wanted in a woman. She loved kissing, loved being held, enjoyed spontaneous sexual tendencies, balled on a budget, and loved dancing and music. This relationship started like a fairytale with all cylinders on go mode. We enjoyed each other's time and space as we would go on outings and watch the world as we held each other, embracing the time as clouds would take footsteps across the sky. We would read together, thinking of things to come once I had gotten my divorce, and we discussed how we would merge our families.

It seemed like time was finally my best friend, but the test happened when adversity came into play. As always, that's when things broke loose. I found myself looking stupid at all the things she asked, and I wondered how I would become compliant with her demands. The crazy part is that she started off understanding the situation, and then she flipped the switch. The problem was money. I got hit with back child support from the state, which froze my assets and secret accounts. She was very knowledgeable about everything, but it felt like she wanted out of the relationship because we were suddenly arguing about stupid shit. Each time, it pushed me away. Finally, she pulled the trigger and said, "Get out!" Now understand that this broke my heart, and when a guy is searching for a replacement in his heart and trying to do all things possible to make this work, it kills his ego and pride that he is pushed away. To add insult to injury, I went to work that day, and my car wouldn't start when I got off. I called my wife to come and pick me up. I was not thinking of anything that had transpired over the last year between us, judging by her quick response. She demonstrated that she felt the same.

She came through, and we went to the crib and had a long talk that night. The kicker comes when the one that kicked you out wants you back. She hit me up, asking me to forgive her intentions. She said we needed to try and work through our issues, but I was upset because regardless of how mad you get, you should never throw your weight around and cut off a person who will change the world for you!

I went to her house to pick up my belongings, and she got physical with me! Even if I wanted to pursue this relationship, her act of physical violence deterred my decision. , I reciprocated what I was putting in the atmosphere with my wife and other women. I had to go back to the drawing board. I tasted some of my adversity, and it broke me down. I was standing across the room from the woman I asked for a divorce, and now I was asking her to forgive me. I told her that I wanted to move forward and try again. Now, it is true that I am an asshole, and I didn't deserve to be in her presence, but I do show flashes of being a good man. I think that, in the end, that was her defining moment. As always, I acted as if nothing had happened, and we tried to start where we left off when the relationship was working.

Now, any guy knows that your lady might have stepped out while you were gone and made a new friend. It is where karma kicks a dog into understanding, so you must not feed someone something you won't eat. I remember listening to my wife talk about this guy friend a lot, which was unusual considering that he wasn't a factor. We were planning a significant change for our family, so my wife, sister, and I took a trip out of state to check and see if this was where we would reside. From the time on the plane and during different incidents, my wife talked about this friend so much that it pissed me off. Then, that voice came, and I had to remember who put him there. What I mean is if this dude fulfilled anything in her personal life, I put him there. Therefore, I had to listen to this woman talk, and when I addressed it, she acted as if there was no interaction between them. I knew, but I had to suck it up due to all I had done over the years. Some things in my closet that I had to understand had been put on the other foot. I vowed to do better with my ignorance, so I wouldn't have to eat that shit again.

We moved forward and started to plan for this life-changing moment as the idea would be for my wife to move first and get established as I settled things and prepared for the move. When she left, I thought about things that didn't matter, and I started thinking with the wrong head. I went out and found myself entertaining the thought of smashing this lady who, in passing, would always throw it out there when we were in the same space. I wanted to go through with this particular time, and she got ready to drop down, but she stopped. Now, I was pissed off for two reasons. First, why would you leave me, your mouth, and cootie cat hanging? Second, I just went back on my vows again, and through all this, I am always asking God for a pass and for Him to forgive me for my transgressions and ignorance. I knew then that change was necessary.

I had to get back on business, so I ended up selling most of the items and giving things away to those in need.

The transition was great and much needed due to my youngest son attending high school in the fall in our new state. He would be better off due to the different atmosphere. We hit a couple of bumps moving down. I always learned to keep my paperwork in order, your name being the most important. I say this because we sometimes find ourselves denied certain luxuries due to needing the correct paperwork for our past financial statements, paychecks, certificates, etc. We got settled, and although my mischief stopped at work, it continued when I went out of state.

I always allowed my dishonesty to become my reality. I was willing to risk it all for someone off the menu. This lady was a friend of a friend, considered off-limits, but I liked to push things to fit my what-if mentality. It is crazy, but here I go again. I was trying to get her to open up and disregard my marriage and what it would do to her friendship. Her loyalty to her friend was more substantial than my pursuit of turning her on. As always, I would go home as if nothing had transpired, and I would get mad when I went through adversity due to my transgressions. I looked in the mirror and was unhappy with myself, knowing I needed to change, but I would say others needed to change. Time would pass, and we would celebrate our 10th anniversary in our favorite place, Jamaica, enjoying ourselves and the family who came along with us. Once we came home a few months later, we would return to a world of ridiculousness due to my sexual hunger. She never wanted me, so why shouldn't I give it to someone who would enjoy me? She would come through the drive-thru and ask a question, and I would reply, and she would smile. It would be the start of something, and I was once again willing to let it all go for a taste of something new. While getting to know each other, we would discover similarities and find mutual things we both loved to indulge in.

My manipulative ways made her the woman she once disliked. We continued complicating matters even though we both knew our spiritual

Father disapproved of our actions. I couldn't stand myself. I was again putting my pleasure and lust before my marriage because I didn't love myself. This time my wife did not stand down. She tried to find a way to talk to this woman face-to-face, but it did not happen, and I was relieved. You never knew what emotion might come out, and I wouldn't have blamed her because it wasn't her fault. It was mine. We escaped that confrontation, but the next one was unavoidable. It was time to answer God. I knew that He disagreed with me breaking my marital vows. I knew I would have to pay for my indiscretions, and so I did, with the exception of losing my job and not knowing which way to go. All I knew was that change was needed.

Chapter 3
The Blame Game

Many factors can cause us to believe it is wise to blame consequences, repercussions, and downfalls on others and the world because you do not want to face what you see in the mirror. While your DNA does play a role in your life, it doesn't define you. Once we find fault in the things we can control, we can determine the outcome of our situations. The journey is authentic from the beginning of the learning stage. I knew what good and evil was based on repeated instructions from my parents. When I did not move, I received a whooping, and when I did as Illustrated, I received a thank you from my mother. As I continued the first five years of my life, I was introduced to the highs and lows of life.

Your decisions will always directly affect your life due to the language and actions displayed in front of you that you will imitate. The language and activities that influence you to include how you pronounce words, the choice of serving and worshiping God and Jesus, how you clean up around yourself, how you speak to others, the understanding of sexuality, and the degree to which you perform well in school. It truly is the molding stage, and when done correctly, it adds to a child's drive to impress mom and dad. We, as people, love to receive some form of recognition, whether positive or negative. The ages of 6 to 10 are crucial because of the habits we develop during those times. We find our self-consciousness and begin understanding different parts of our body and hidden abilities that start to become evident.

Life has a lot of factors that control your behaviors at this age. Based on my life and those around me that I have studied, 60% is by sight.

We emulate what's happening in front of us, especially if it is repetitive. Depending on the atmosphere in which we were raised, we tend to gravitate toward negative things faster than positive ones. 30% of our behavior is influenced by hearing. This analogy comes from seeing the action first, listening to the vocabulary that comes from it, sorting it out, and deciding to ignore or follow it.

These were things that I faced in the home and out on the streets that molded us into that 10% that impacts us doing what we feel. We understand between the ages of 10 to 15 that; we are making life-enhancing decisions or facing death. My reference to death is any place where your soul is obsolete such as jail, life in prison, or the release of the spirit from the body. It represents game over.

I remember this time frame being the most critical time in my life. We were in a new neighborhood with which I wasn't familiar, and I still blamed my father for us losing our house due to his ignorance. Everything I saw and heard was about to be applied in this time frame. I remember dreaming about being an athlete. I knew I had the physical traits to be great, but I didn't have anyone to train me. I made some new friends, and I discovered new things. I speculated about stuff around me. I wanted to play basketball, but I did not practice enough, and when it came time to try out, I didn't make the team. I blamed it on the coach and my height.

Nothing can stop someone who practices what they are trying to accomplish. You have to believe and listen to others when given feedback. I became a procrastinator on things that would change my future and gave energy to something I wanted but didn't necessarily need. It only got me closer to being lost in my fantasy and using women as my outlet. I would continue doing things that took away everything, like officially wanting to join a gang. I studied the laws and creeds as if they would elevate me in society. What it caused me to understand was that if you don't play by the rules, you cripple the system's strength. I would meet a lot of great brothers of the struggle and listen to ideas and things they would love to change. It gave me the opinion never to box myself in, and I always understood what you give up if you get caught.

No matter what, if I did it or was a part of something, no snitching was allowed. How can you agree to do something and get caught and tell someone else to reduce your time or get someone else killed? That's why I learned what type of people I had around me at an early age, and I almost lost it all going somewhere I should not have been. I was listening to someone who honestly didn't know what I was doing, and of course, when it happened, I blamed them when I decided not to go and found a different route to my destination. I believe you will pay for what you do to others when you least expect it, and I did. Time was flying. I had a son and a daughter whom I very seldom saw, and because I did not visualize myself in a dream job or prepare for one, I found myself lost. Man, if the father I had would have been a man and guided me, I would not be in this predicament. I can partially blame myself because my mother tried explaining things, but I chose not to listen. Most of all, what happened to me thus far was never my fault.

Blaming others for my downfall became a habit, hindering me for a while.

I called it a blessing when we ventured out of the city to the suburbs and found a new stomping ground. I started working and soon applied my street mentality to my work ethic. I would learn business in the restaurant field, which was the same as the block without arrests, fights, and gun battles. Fast food is still a drug and becomes an addiction if you don't pace yourself because you love the taste. I had a consistent cash flow and started to meet different connections to separate outlets. I was trying to be better than before and move differently, but I was not optimistic about my direction. I was trying to get into the stock market by listening to someone who came through, but I did not understand how the money flows. I would throw some money away, which was why I discovered that I had to research before investing my money. Of course, I blamed the guy for my loss, but the funny part is that when he said pulling out of the market was best, all I saw was money, and it crashed, and I lost everything. No one taught me about the other side of the business, but with each fall, I would get up.

We eventually got a bachelor's pad, and with the three of us working, we figured that it shouldn't be a problem. Ha! When you go in with someone, ensure the whole block doesn't have access to your home. You already know things are going to come up missing. I blamed them and learned it was my fault for not looking at the big picture: their family members were helping us. It was convenient because I had the money and credentials to have my own space. I kept hitting my head trying to fit in, knowing that the things I did base on assumptions never worked out. I remember thinking that the Internet would not be a successful investment, and when they were looking for investors, I laughed and made a stupid comment. This assumption would cost me millions. I would have to lose again to win. Taking this road is good if you can process what you learned from this.

The big picture is that I am still alive. My kids' mothers are doing their best, and I am broke from spending like no tomorrow. Amid all this, I lost my job at McDonald's due to laziness. I was tasked with cleaning a machine, and because I was doing what I wanted, I ignored my responsibility until I was fired. We ran to unemployment. We felt we could find another job just as fast, paying more if we learned from our mistakes, but it's always easy to blame someone else. Now, the ladies in my life weren't working out, consequent to them not supplying all my needs. It felt like all of them together would have made the perfect woman. Reality check – I did not know who I was and had no purpose other than fitting in with the boys' conversation on how many ladies I hit. This same stupidity caused me to miss out on my true investment—Her.

The reset button was hit. I asked God for a

second chance at life, and I asked Him to send me someone to guide me and teach me how to be a man.

I would return to the store where I first started, where there are new owners, Mr. and Mrs. O'Keefe and their three sons. Growing up, we sometimes become brainwashed by what we hear about other cultures. It is important to never judge a book by its cover. This relationship would start with an understanding that a husband and wife have built their lives and invested time into their business. I shared and respected them because Mrs. O'Keefe was thoughtful and business savvy. She always knew how to get her way. Mrs. Okeefe knew how to do all the little things to make things work. For example, she would decorate for all holidays, always thinking of new ways to bring more guests in and making new items to add to the menu. She pushed the envelope on innovation and made it happen. She was always thinking of ways to maximize productivity and profitability. Now, Mr. O'Keefe was the person who understood all machines, as well as people, and he knew how to put himself in the best position possible when it came to negotiations on their future. They were a genuine power couple, and I would find myself starting to learn what that missing piece was I needed to progress. I listened but did not take notes, leading me only to remember bits and pieces of information. For example, I should have asked what level of commitment and sacrifice was needed instead of asking how they made money.

I put more time into my job than I did my family. My son's mother and I were trying to work on our relationship, although I was still dishonest. I was making excuses and blaming anything that went wrong on her. I tried my best to build a firm foundation with my family and assisted in any way I could. It felt like how a family was supposed to be. I pushed myself to listen more and show better progress at work. I was moved up and shined like a star because I gave all I had. However, my home relationship would suffer and eventually break. If you asked me, I felt she was cheating anyway because we only had sex once. I thought That's not my baby; she better stop playing. The cheater always feels that way but never sees what they do as wrong.

Work was going great, but I was thirsty for someone to fill her spot, so like any lost dog, I was looking for a home. I found myself acting like a doorknob, where everyone got a turn. I eventually returned to my relationship with my son's mother and tried a little better because I had four kids. I envisioned myself being a good husband and father, but the lust in me wouldn't change. My job was excellent. I was head of the store and felt empowered. However, like anything that doesn't have a person's total commitment, it's only temporary. The relationship continued, but I dealt with someone this time. I considered the what-ifs, and as usual, things were going great until this person said something that made me understand that I didn't give myself time to heal and get over her.

We hit a massive bump at work. I won a trip to the Olympics to represent the brand. The gift was taken from me and given to my coworker.

The owners did this because they felt it was unfair to the previous general manager, who was never offered this opportunity. It built a wedge in my relationship with my leaders. The grudge I held interfered with my job in a significant way. I moved back home and hoped my wife would stop the relationship she had. Now, the shoe was on the other foot. This guy was treating her better than I was, but the difference was that she knew one day I would get it together. She was willing to try and forget him. I was getting hit from all sides. Home and work were both driving me crazy because neither was balanced. My house was unbalanced because when you leave your space and move into a home where it is a free for all, people will steal and abuse your kindness.

My kids suffered because I was not leading by example, and I would come home and not pay attention to them because I was tired. Sadly, I always pushed them away. Even though my wife was also tired, she tried to do what she could when she came home. Our kids were self-sufficient when it came to school, thanks to her. We went through our ups and downs but decided to stick it out this time. I was just doing enough and not pushing myself anymore like before, and I still cheated with ladies in my work vicinity. I was "Mr. Can't Get It Together." I found myself lying to myself and would jump out there because I wanted to stop. I asked her to marry me, and she said yes. I was surprised but happy because she always had my heart. I didn't know what love was, although I said the word. Even though I felt as if I didn't know what it was, I still desired it.

Mr. and Mrs. Okeefe was happy for me. The conversations and advice felt great, so I pushed myself to improve. The sad part is that I was still cheating, as was my wife-to-be. We were looking in the mirror and not being truthful with each other. She was still putting herself in the space of a dude, and I was just trying to feel wanted.

We invited family members from across the United States, and the money spent was nonrefundable.

My little sister loved my wife-to-be, and she was happy to see us get married, so I had to relinquish all other opportunities and move forward.

Whatever is done in the dark comes to light. The marriage license got misplaced. We both blamed each other, and we were about to have a fallout before and after the wedding. I took the blame to ease the tension. We had a beautiful wedding, and the reception was lit with an open bar.

We got home, and my wife didn't want to be with me. It caused a problem between us on our first marriage day because I only had 3 hrs to sleep and had to get ready for a picnic. I would be stuck cooking and setting up the whole day. I had the time of my life, and our families enjoyed themselves together. We would try to get back on track when we went on our honeymoon, but it was as if she were somewhere else. The affection felt like a lack of effort, so I wondered if I had made the best choice. Once I returned to work, one of the ladies I was dealing with was upset because I got married, or at least that's what I blamed it on. I had lied to her and broke her heart, so she told Mr. Okeefe she had given me five-hundred dollars. He called me into the office and explained his disappointment in me, and told me he would be giving her money back. We had words, but I respected him because he was trying to teach me how to be a man, but instead, I would remain a boy.

Things started to roll downhill. I lost my two uncles, and the biggest hit was losing my baby sister due to health complications. My world felt like it shut down for a minute. My wife and I were still trying to get it on track, and then I went and crossed the lines again, lusting for physical connection and conversation in my head space. I made excuses for why I did it, but it would turn into an ongoing thing that would almost cost me everything.

The sad part is that when I was in jail on my first anniversary for chasing nothing, the one I risked losing, "my wife" came and bailed me out.

I would lie about the truth because that's what a liar and cheater are accustomed to doing and because who I saw in the mirror was eating me up. Like any drug addict, I would return to smoking weed only to realize that my reality was still there. I sometimes wanted to give up and die, but I was given a reason to proceed with life each time. Being out in those streets was reckless. There was no protection from sexual death, mental suicide, and death by violence. The only reason I was still alive was my family's prayers. My wife had more faith than I did, but if you let me tell you, I was better than her because I went to church now and then. I was still a heathen though. Around this time my job was falling apart and the trust factor was depleting as now my license was suspended for my infraction, and I had limited work hours. I wanted to operate as if nothing ever happened. I was always willing to give everyone else advice but not listen to myself. I knew those same people were prospering while I remained in the same place.

My home life was stressful because my wife's family members unknowingly dealt drugs to an undercover cop in front of the house. The police hit us with $15,000 worth of violations and lied about why they needed to enter our home. This ended up working in our favor because they violated our rights. As a result, the fine was reduced to $3500.

I was stressed out and didn't feel like smoking this time, so I took a drive. Unfortunately I returned to my old ways and ended up in the backseat with a new woman. I would hide my face when I came home each time because of the guilt. It was time to depart and leave because I didn't want to change or admit fault, so I let go of the best place for me and would regret walking away. The grass isn't greener on the other side is an original notation, especially when you leave things the wrong way.

My next job was a nightmare. I had to deal with an investigation of the theft of a missing deposit the second week. The general manager that was training me was untrustworthy and it wasn't a coincidence that someone was looking for her regarding money. The investigation would lead to a written warning for me and her. She knew the angles of the camera and would go out with a back injury leaving me to run the store. I worked 264 days straight with no day off killing overtime. My wife paying the bills was great, but always helping her family out with our money really made me angry. This would cause conflict in my mind towards my wife because they never appreciated what we did. We would go on vacation to Vegas and have a great time, and then when we came home, we had another issue. Problems at work and at home just kept on proceeding as if the world was against me.

Things at the job just started to fall apart my boss and I couldn't avoid confrontation. Because of this, I was terminated. I blamed it all on him because he was a young dummy, but in reality, I was going through issues at home and work and could not balance the workload, so I forgot to do my job 70% of the time. I was still cheating and knew why things were not going my way because I chose to do what I wanted and not change. I found a new job but I still hadn't looked in the mirror and corrected my selfish ways in my marriage. I still did not want to blame myself for the lack of my success.

I did not want to cheat at work, but I eventually did. My wife and I had issues because I wanted her to be more affectionate. I hated that it felt like I was the only one who wanted to be sexual. It was a recurring issue throughout our marriage, and this is the blame I used to propel me to cheat. I told her I loved her but was not in love with her. Because of this, I walked away again. My wife was willing to divorce me, but I had to pay for it, and around this time, I fell back into financial hardship due to being ignorant about a child support order. I lost my money to pay for this order. Because I decided to have a pity party, I found myself in Wonderland with another woman, and of course, everything is excellent in the beginning but the bottom always drops out in the end. I was sold a dream at work about the direction in which they would like the business to go only to see total chaos. I was trying to find myself. I should have gone where it all started and hit the reset button, but my ego and pride wouldn't let me. God is always watching over us, and I wanted to share my faith in Jesus with my wife. I finally tried to be consistent, and things started to look up. God opened a door, allowing me to move my job to another state. We decided to make it happen.

Things in the house took a turn for the worst as one member chose to cosign for a family member who wasn't trustworthy. It would cause legal action to be brought against the property. Through the grace and mercy of God, things eventually worked out for the best. I vowed I would do better with my faith and actions as a believer and changed as we moved to a new state. I decided to embrace new things to be appreciative of as we started to move forward with opportunities in front of us.

I would enjoy listening to my wife become more open to communicating with others and stepping outside of her stale and stubborn ways. We began to gel and converse with each other and this led to more intimacy. It carried on for quite some time. At the time, I had three of my kids staying with me, and my daughter was having issues because she did not want to listen to anyone. Conceptually, we blamed it on the person that raised her or whomever she was around. The unfortunate part was that I was doing me, so how could I be mad at how she felt? Because of unfortunate miscommunications, she eventually moved back home.

My new job started perfectly. As time progressed, I began to help train staff members on the correct procedures, and that's when the problem occurred. I was accused of things that never happened, and HR was told I was rude to one of the managers. Naturally, this caused a ripple in the store because the general manager couldn't look at my face due to her not telling the truth.

I would go on and pray for a change and that's when God blessed me. My wife and I would be with each other because we worked nearby. I was doing good in the relationship for the most part until I went to Chicago and put myself in a spot where I would think with the wrong head. I was trying to seduce my ex-girlfriend's buddy and was upset that she wasn't going. I constantly disrespected my female relationships at this time, but I am glad she rejected me. So the relationship at home would take another turn due to my sister-in-law moving in. I agreed for her to move in with us even though I knew that I wasn't mentally all together at the time. It created a wedge between my wife and me as time progressed, and I became tired of being married to her family. My supervisor and I formed a bond at work that helped me grow in many ways. Together we raised the store sales and ran better profit controllable. I soon moved forward. My mindset grew, and I attended church more and tried to lead by example for my family. My wife's father was ill then, and I didn't want to do anything that would cause pain anymore. Based on my performance, things began to improve, and brand changes were being discussed. I later moved to another workspace that needed to be upgraded. Unfortunately, this plan did not fall through because my friend died from health complications. It affected the way the brand was being promoted. I was blessed to receive some help from a young man whom I can trust to this present day.

My marriage started to shift again, and not for good. I found myself back at square one. I wanted to walk away from everything. There was craziness in my household, marriage, and mind. I cheated again and didn't care how it affected anyone. I broke the rules at work and became less of a leader.

Usually, I would blame everyone around me, but this time, the blame was on me. "Always put God, Jesus, and the Holy Spirit first to have a true relationship—not religion."

Chapter 4
From a Boy to a Man

My definition of a boy is a follower of anything that feels fun and believes they should never suffer the consequences for their wrongdoings. A boy is selfish and never considers that he is wrong. A boy also lies, cheats, deceives, and never leads by example. As I illustrated before, growing up without an active father in your life causes a boy to be clueless about his journey to manhood. There are Basic Instructions Before Leaving Earth (Bible) that you can read and follow to get on the right path that would be best for you. In my case, I had to hit my head almost 100 times before I got anything right. Most of us become what we see until we can make our own decisions. I would always tell myself that I would never be like my father, but the truth is that I have some of his ways. I was supposed to pay attention and ensure my kids were hugged and kissed whenever I saw them. It didn't happen because I was too tired to do so.

One of the things I knew was that I had a sense of compassion for others. I would always find myself trying to help someone regardless of how they treated me. It was because my mother's family assisted us while growing up. After losing our home, things became difficult because I still wasn't clear on how my father quickly lost his money. I have never seen my dad apologize without being intoxicated, and he had the nerve to say he was a man. At a certain point, I began to shut people out who weren't providing structure. My mother would talk about what needed to happen and what she wanted to see her sons accomplish, but it went in one ear and out the other. Some male teachers in high school tried to teach me how to be a man, but at that time, my penis was running my life.

The words *commitment, communication,* and *consistency* were a foundation that I built for myself and used for harmful purposes. Being premeditated always allowed me to stay one step ahead of the craziness around me and in me.

I would find myself using the 3 C's regarding women and the understanding of gang involvement. Life will teach you many lessons if you allow these things to consume you.

Sexually transmitted diseases, fights, broken hearts, kids, and death were all a part of the equation when dealing with certain women. Gang fights, jail, prison, killings, homelessness, drug addiction, brokenness, and death were all consequences of choosing to be in a gang.

You are the only one who can "pick your poison." The head of these gangs were boys leading boys, and lives were constantly lost. I experienced flashes of death throughout this time, doing what those around me were doing. But I knew this wasn't what I wanted, and there was more. I've seen how happy others are and wanted it for me.

We never had a solid plan whenever I discussed anything with the team. We only had short-term goals with no long-term payout.

We served our family members, and certain gang members stole from each other and blamed it on the cluckers. I listened to the people moving amongst the thieves and learned the politics of the streets of Chicago. It was fueled by nothing more than greed.

How does this relate to becoming a man? If you are not paying attention, you could get caught up in this life and suffer the consequences. I've always wanted to become a good husband and father but didn't know the required work ethic.

I tried to get back on track with this other young lady by having an monogamous relationship, only later to find out that she wanted a threesome while we were together. It did nothing but turn me back to my old ways. I decided to be a better man with the new woman

I was dating. I was ready to do everything correctly with her until I shared my intentions with someone I thought was my friend. I allowed him to convince me that I wasn't ready to settle down and that I wasn't a pimp anymore. I didn't propose to her and later discovered that this person gave her false information about my doings. When you hang around boys, you act like them.

I eventually moved around but still dealt with these characters and asked myself why. I remember looking in the mirror and thinking that I needed to change.

I finally got caught up in a one-day fling with an old girlfriend I couldn't have kids with when we were together. She later told me she was pregnant, which started our relationship as friends again. During this time, abortions were being administered because I didn't understand how vital my name was when I laid down with these women to plant my seed. I learned how much these women had to endure simply because I did not want to step up. I wanted my son's mother and me to work, so we moved in together. I would adjust and try to improve, and while my little sister was happy to see us together, I still did not understand my role. I ensured that I gave her what she asked for in terms of monetary contribution. I found myself back at home with my mother, and this was a place that I vowed never to return to. I eventually ended up being blessed with my spot. I was trying to be a one-woman man again, only to almost have to knock out my new girl ex-boyfriend. I had to leave her because she still desired him. While I had other women to entertain, none wanted to change their hustles. I liked that they were getting money but at what cost?

My kids meant the world to me. I would spend time with them, but I could have done more. I did just enough to meet my standards. They only wanted a consistent father, but I was too caught up in my emotions.

My ex and I moved in together again but decided to go our separate ways when I found her in an undergarment that she had no explanation for. We walked away only to find out that she was pregnant. Because of this, we tried to reconcile our differences and try again. My mother said I needed Jesus, so I read the Bible verses she and my dad read to mend their relationship. I forgave my father for his transgressions, only for him to disappear with a crackhead from work and break our hearts and hope of me seeing a true transformation. It killed my understanding because the DNA that runs through my veins is troubled, and I wanted to know how to break the curse. I started trying to be more understanding of her feelings. Around this time, my little sister was sick, and my son's mother was there to assist. I was very grateful to her during this time.

We decided to buy a house together with her father. I knew going in that there would be things I might not like, so in my mind, this would be temporary. During this time, I got to know her father and tried to garner as much wisdom from him as possible. After getting to know him, I learned that he never knew how to respect his significant other but did his best to care for his kids. I didn't get any insight from him, and we broke up again as time progressed. I would leave but still assist with my sons to the best of my ability. I should have given myself time to move on once we went our separate ways. The next woman I selected was a good friend, and I should have prepared my heart for her at that time because something simple made me walk away, which wasn't right. What I am learning is that I have the answer to my problems. I just should follow my advice. I finally took my advice and said I would make RERE my wife no matter what happened.

I believed that this was the right thing to do. The wedding was one of the most beautiful things I had participated in. We would rewrite vows "for worse or for better" due to my indiscretions. I was a compulsive liar because my actions did not align with what was said. I could have written all of R. Kelly's apology songs because I treated her heart like a revolving door.

I sometimes wrote down all the crazy things in the relationship, but I couldn't see my fault because of my ego and pride. This is why I wrote the story the way I did and left out most of what I did back then.

I was dishonest with myself, and this caused me to be dishonest with her. She stayed with my little sister until her death, and I had the nerve to question her love and affection. I should have questioned my loyalty to her and why I always found a way to walk away.

I saw what I needed to do and sacrificed for her when necessary, but it wasn't appreciated. I bought her a new car, but it wasn't what she wanted. She was not overly excited. I hated the fact that she wasn't appreciative. I would buy her flowers from time to time and still received the same response. When I received no response to being a better man, I gave way and went back into my shell. It's vital that, as partners, you have to be thankful for both the little and big things. We both reached a point where we wanted to take the step forward to change, so we took the necessary steps. We both prayed that our marriage would be strengthened and that we genuinely displayed love all the time. We knew that we were going to have to work hard for this. We knew we would have to let go of each other's pasts, which was hard. I couldn't stand that she didn't want to fight for our relationship, so I started using profanity to make my point.

As a kid, the devil would always attack me with the falling off the cliff dream or scare me when alone in the dark. It felt like I couldn't talk or call out to anyone during those times, but once I found God, it stopped. I am imperfect and struggled with many things, but never my faith.

We recently celebrated our tenth anniversary and enjoyed ourselves. We even exchanged rings. I wished I had spent more time realizing how I was brought up and the tendencies I was introduced to in my surroundings. Remembering how your significant other was raised is essential in any relationship. It plays a fundamental role in communication, finances, and everything else. It allows you to understand the tasks as a couple to work on before saying, "I do." Once we returned home, I felt something was different in my spirit.

I suppressed my feelings and refused to be honest with myself. It would cause me to tilt again and start to dismantle my family.

My sister Kesha had always been there for me when I needed a different perspective. I would always listen but only take some of her advice into consideration. This was because I wanted to hear what I wanted to hear. I was upfront about my infidelity this time and where I was in the relationship. I was tired of many things, and I never put them on a scale of 1 to 10 to see how they affected the relationship. I never thought about what we could do to work through them as a team. I had just begun to see things differently but never let go of my pride, so changing my ways for the better was challenging. My conscience knew that something was off, and I always went to church whenever I needed answers to life's questions. You have to be in the Bible to receive the message, and at that time, I was not. I started listening to more gospel music and even practiced refraining from using profanity. It was what I liked to call my spiritual dialysis. I began to see a change in some things I did, but I was careless with the things that mattered the most, like my integrity. The lies started to eat me up, and I took myself and the woman I was dating to a church where God revealed our next step as believers. What is evident is that sinning is not winning. You can do what you please but will pay for it in this life or the next. You must own the words you speak. When you take vows, you must honor what you say in the relationship and understand that nothing is worth having without a work ethic and commitment.

Chapter 5
The New Michael Evans

April 16, 2017, would change my life and start my journey of becoming a Man of God. On this day, the woman I was with at the time attended a church service at Friendship Baptist Church of the Colony, where The Senior Pastor, Rev. Gregory C. Trotter, preached, and I felt he was speaking directly to me. The choir sang a song selection by Antony Brown that I had been listening to for the past three weeks; *"You Thought I Was Worth Saving."* It felt as if I was supposed to be there. I was sitting next to my Aunt Mary, a church member, and throughout the sermon, I would shed tears of redemption hearing the gospel speak to me.

That day we both understood what needed to happen and that if we continued on the same path, nothing good would happen for us in this relationship. I ended up calling my wife, and in a disrespectful tone, I told her that God was making me come home! That night he sent me a message directing me to apologize to my wife and correct the way I spoke his name in vain. Although she was still upset about what happened, we attended my cousin's birthday party the following weekend and enjoyed ourselves. I started to drive for Uber, which was the best thing I had ever done. That first week I drove her to and from work. I ensured we had lunch together, and after work, we would go and see her father, who wasn't doing so well. Each time he saw his baby girl, he would light up. It was an inspiration for me to know the level of dedication she displayed for those whom she loved. I wrote down my relationship goals for myself which were necessary as I worked on being a better friend to myself and learning how to love myself. I wrote on a sheet of paper all the dark things I have done or experienced in this life thus far and all the good things I have done for myself and others. I'd pick one habit, break it in 21 days, and remove it within three months. I also started the ten and ten, which is when you identify ten things you love and dislike about yourself. It became the tool I implemented during couples counseling as I tried to perfect my life change.

As time passed, my wife's father passed away, and even though she was hurting, she remained humble and trusted God that her heart had prepared her for this day. Sadly, when someone passes away, family members always want to know about an insurance policy they never contributed to. Although it was hard, we moved forward from this and enjoyed our beautiful anniversary in Chicago, where our life first started. Looking across the dinner table, I could feel her heart wondering if I had changed. I would smile at her and ask her to write down things she wanted me to change in our relationship this time. She replied I don't want

you to be what I want you to be." "I want you to
be what's in your heart." I prayed to our Father
God and asked him to guide me, and I reached
out to my mother, a God-fearing woman, to ask
where I should start in the Bible to grasp my
faith better. The *First Epistle of John 2:15-18*
would change my life and redeem my spirit. I
joined the church under the leadership of Pastor
Trotter, who guided me to understand that I am
important, necessary, and needed. As I started
completing my task of redemption, my spirit
began to administer to my guest, who was going
through what I had just overcome. I thank God
and Jesus, Our Lord and Savior, who allowed me
to understand my why in the storm. I found my
compassion, commitment, and consistency
illustrated through the scriptures in the Bible.
My wife has been strong since her father's
passing, and I thank God for allowing me to be
there for her. We would enjoy date night even
more now that we have a foundation in our
marriage. The relationship feels excellent on all
levels. My spirituality, finances, and lovemaking

are in order, and it feels good to love Rechelle Evans properly. Preparing with her each morning for work, getting her the things she needs before she goes to work, having lunch with her, opening the car door when she gets in, and kissing her once she reaches her destination is priceless. I am doing the things that are necessary for the relationship. I am using the Bible to teach me how to be a better husband and man. Which revealed that to become a great leader, you must be a great servant of God's will and lead by example. *Matthew 6:33* But seek ye first the kingdom of God, and his righteousness; and all these things shall be added unto you. I see her better now that I have started to trust in God, Jesus, and the Holy Spirit because now I understand what was being shown to me all these years later.

When I cried out for a purpose to live and change, He gave me a son by my wife. She was always there through both the good and bad. A real man couldn't ask for more. She was never the issue. I was always the issue because I didn't understand what loyalty meant. Now I live to serve God and fulfill her Needs. Our days together are heartfelt because we care about each other and what happens during our days. I have stopped edging God out (EGO) and being prideful because the teaching has shown me why becoming a humble servant is crucial to see the covenant of our Lord and Savior, Jesus Christ. Because of my testimony, I have been able to lead others to Christ. *1 Peter 5:9 Whom resist, steadfast in faith, knowing that the same afflictions are accomplished in your brethren that are in the world.*

2017 was a mixture of ups and downs. We celebrated with the elders of my family during December, and this would be the last time we would all be together, as many of them passed away and some members grew apart. When my wife's father passed, I knew I had to step up and become the man she needed me to be. I joined the church and transitioned from being a boy to a man. I finally apologized to my children for my absence in their life. I am hopeful that they will forgive me and we can move forward. I have taken the necessary steps to build my relationships on hope, faith, and love. My life journey has inspired me to write this book to help people understand that it is ok to change.

I began writing my one-year, three-year, and five-year goals to succeed. I asked God to allow me and my wife to become homeowners after a year. I then asked God to give me the strength to remain monogamous and become a mentor for young men and women. I finally asked God to cover me with his blood so that I could become a better husband, father, leader, and servant to Jesus Christ and my family. I started a new job through God's grace and faced much adversity. The blessing is that I now have God in my life, and things have become easier to deal with at work because I can focus on the task. I was so happy to have my mother live with us, especially since she had issues with my brother. Because of this, we could seek refuge in our relationship with each other and the Bible. The apartment where we lived was a lesson learned because it taught me never to depend on others to repair things. I was balanced at home and work. As our finances grew, we finally started the process of home shopping. It felt great, and things were looking up.

My youngest son attended prom and graduated. My play son KP got married, and we were finally approved for the house we wanted in the neighborhood of our choice. When God is the head, nothing is impossible. The housewarming was fantastic because my wife was glowing and finally happy. Things tried to take a turn for the worse when my oldest son was in an accident, but thankfully he was covered by the blood and was unharmed. My wife and I took a much-needed trip to Punta Cana together. Our marriage had done a complete 180, and it was due to God's grace and mercy, and I was happy we were in a better place. Instead of saying the word love, I now demonstrate it. Punta Cana was like a second Honeymoon, and it made me happy to see my wife playful and enjoying life. We were in awe of each other and amazed at how far we had come.

In 2018 my wife had surgery, and my mother-in-law stayed with us while she recovered. My wife is a strong woman, and her strength always amazes me. In 2019 we started the year off by fasting for God and Jesus and receiving the instructions to read the Bible in a year. I was excited to be closer to my wife, family, God, Jesus, and the Holy Spirit. This very foundation is what strengthened our marriage. I learned that all things are possible through Christ, who strengthens me. As I look in the mirror, I have been consistently dedicated to the Bible for two years, and things have improved through my faith. My tendencies at work have changed, my lust for the flesh has been depleted, and my unhealthy habits are slowly fading. I love what I see in the mirror and am beginning to say my name with confidence, dignity, and purpose. Establishing ownership in everything with your name is imperative, for God gave you this. I am no longer talking about what I am going to do. I lead with intent and action by asking God what he wants me to do.

I now have a support system that holds me accountable for being a better husband, father, and leader. My wife and I now plan things together, duplicate bank accounts, and ensure that trust is the foundation for our relationship. Work is now enjoyable, and I took the wisdom and knowledge from my former work leaders Mr. and Mrs. Okeefe. My new leader also provides excellent insight and expertise to add to my repertoire. Gina is significant because she always treats me as family, which is needed in all business relationships. Looking back at the situation when my mom moved in, she was unhealthy. Knowing everything in her system is better, and now she is missing home isn't an issue because I enjoyed our conversations about God and Jesus.

I feel empowered through her teachings and know that I am self-sufficient now. I also reconnected with my youngest daughter, and my wife and I took our two oldest grandchildren to Walt Disney World. We had a blast and felt fortunate just to make these things happen. We enjoyed another anniversary celebration in which love was in the air. My 45th birthday with family and friends was one of the greatest because my wife made it happen. I vowed to keep preparing for what GOD has in store for us.

Christmas time was crazy because it was then that we realized how many grandchildren we truly have. My wife and I vowed to give our grandkids everything we never had. I wanted 2020 to be the year everything came together, but things seemed to go downhill. This was due to our society not having enough faith. As you become closer to God, you can see those who read and think and those who don't. God has always been God; you must believe and know that He can do anything.

To see people being more ignorant than ever before, with so many people questioning whether there is a God due to what man has done, is preposterous. My faith is more substantial than I see in society based on their actions, so excuse me if I don't watch the news or listen to the radio. God does not want us to operate in the spirit of fear. God wants us to trust him. It caused arguments with many people, but I did not care because I knew what He brought me through. He said this too shall pass, and I believe in His word because of His grace and mercy. If it is my time to die, I am happy to say I have experienced real love. I am sharing God's love.

I still shook hands, prayed, and hugged those in need. We celebrated life with every chance we had together in my house. We visited our grandchildren and would come home and have a family get-together. I have never seen so many people afraid because of what was told.

Then to add insult to injury, we are supposed to be one nation under God, but every chance we get, we show a different belief system and wonder why we are losing momentum. There is always a lesson to be learned in every situation.

I was getting baptized again, which allowed me to feel the weight of my past fall off like heavy baggage and walk by faith, not sight. Having a chance to empty my closet to my wife was a blessing, and her not allowing it to define our marriage was God's grace and mercy. Once I completed my three year goal, my staff surprised me with my first-ever Manniversary celebration. I looked in the mirror and started crying tears of joy because of the change in my life. I don't have to call myself a man because it shows in everything I do. My wife and I celebrated another anniversary, and it was extra special to me because of the growth God allowed us to see.

My mother will be going home soon, and I am glad I was able to provide for her as she wanted. 2020 was a blessing as I accomplished my 3-year goal. I now have three years of Bible study under my belt, which I can feel, and the best part is that marriage is wonderful.

The year 2021 started with a significant loss. My cousin (sister) Kesha lost her father. I flew to Chicago to attend the funeral and support my family.

I was faced with work challenges due to management changes. It felt like a dictatorship because of the lack of communication. Over these last couple of years, my wife has lost some important people in her life, and the blessing is to see her still smile throughout these rough and trying times. I ended up quitting my job, and my spirit told me to go and see my uncle, whom I hadn't seen in about five years. I took the trip, and we made some great memories in Chicago on our road trip for that day. I started a new job but wasn't happy with the leadership. I decided to make it work. Culture is everything in any establishment, and I believe that any stressful environment has to have a foundation built on internal guests and external guests. An internal guest has to see the leader demonstrate the qualities being asked of that person. It builds trust and understanding. No one sees me slacking because there is always something to do, and I practice what I preach. This is how I continuously set the bar for myself.

I witnessed a miracle guided by the hands. I watched a car slide into a ditch on the right side of the expressway and flip four times one way and reverse-flip four times in the other direction. The car finally flipped out of the ditch and landed on the driver's door. I immediately assisted the young lady with getting out of the car with no visible injuries. God is real. I never question my faith.

One of the most incredible things to happen was a birthday breakfast with my father and brothers. He turned 70; this was the first time we all sat down and had breakfast together. It was indeed a blessing. My wife and I revisited San Antonio for our anniversary and loved being in each other's space again. She is truly a beautiful woman inside and out. We were in the moment and would take a trip with the family to celebrate our Godmother Ann's 70th birthday in Jamaica. We had a blast, but during this trip, I slipped up and forgot who I work for and what I represent. I was over-intoxicated and not being the best husband, which prompted my wife to say, *"We are both on vacation, not just you."*

I realized that she was right and came back down to earth. There were more celebrations lined up. We would attend our little cousin's sweet sixteen, 90's themed birthday party. I also celebrated Momma Mathis' 75th birthday, which was a blessing. She has been the one that has shown me unconditional love, as well. 2021 had come to a close. Although we had some great moments, I was slipping.

The God we serve always allows the necessary things to happen to his servants. My wisdom and faith are more substantial, and I always pray for everyone. At one point, I wanted to backslide and participate in some of my old habits. Temptation is strong, but I've learned to surround myself only with good people. I have to lead with intention.

Never reconnect with people that can't respect you as a married person. That devil slid in briefly, almost costing me everything, but I overcame the temptation.

I would learn of The closing of my first job at Woodfield Mall McDonald's. It was a blessed celebration in which all the bad and good made me understand life and showed me how always to adjust and change if I choose. Time was flying as I came home. I had to prepare to leave again for las vegas to celebrate my mother's 70th birthday and my daughter's 28th birthday. It was the first time the Vickers and Evans families were out of town together. We had a ball. It was indeed a blessing and a lesson learned again for me. My aunt Dorothy came and kept my mother company which I wish I had better planned for. I finally understood why the trip with my uncle was so crucial as he passed away. He taught me a lot, and I thank God for my Uncle Joe being in my life. It made things so much more significant about this life because as we grow older, death becomes more evident.

This year was my wife's milestone birthday year. I was supposed to buy her a new truck, but she preferred to have all ten of our grandchildren and our children gather to celebrate with her. Through the grace of God, He allowed it to happen. It made her very happy, and I had to count my blessings because I never knew my grandparents. I love that we sacrifice for the people that are important to us. We took pictures, enjoyed family time, and took them to Legoland. As their PaPa, I enjoyed seeing and installing structures within them. We have to install in them the correct way to respect each other. As they all left to go back home, we had other visitors come in, and we were surprised and caught off guard, but we simply readjusted our mindset. I counted down the days until our first vacation, which was a 7-day cruise.

We went to celebrate my sister Kesha's birthday with other family members. This cruise was the first one that my wife and I had been on together. I treated her like the Queen she was, and we had a great time. On the second vacation, we went to Cabo San Lucas. My brothers, Tracey, Pat, and sister, Pam, celebrated birthdays. I am always amazed when we can come together as a family for vacations. It is the best experience with family. Seeing new love blossom in the family is a beautiful feeling.

I keep giving God the glory because I could not have experienced this life without his grace and mercy. We came home and prepared for Thanksgiving. My Aunt Mary was sick, so we wrapped her in our prayers.

I was happy to witness my sister-in-law and her two daughters preparing Thanksgiving dinner. It was a blessing to see. You could feel the hope, faith, and love we built in our house. The greatest gift in any holiday is each other; regardless of the past, be in the moment. Christmas was a blessing as we would see our nephew for the first time in almost sixteen years.

Regardless of what you see or go through, if you have faith, all things are possible.

I ended up conversing with my wife about her feelings toward our marriage. She solidified her trust in our relationship. We both are looking forward to more of this new thing. I am happy to report that I also met my 5-year goal. Now, the sky's the limit.

Prayer is the glue to all families around the world. We fail when we forget our greatest weapon against anxiety, racism, infidelity, fear, depression, and everything that deprives us as people. His name is Jesus.

Thoughts and Inspiration

These pages are the thoughts that carried me throughout this journey. God gave me wisdom, and I found helpful advice to tell myself as I prepare for where God is sending me. My goal is to create an understanding of the purpose of transition from a boy to a man. You, too, will celebrate your MANNIVERSARY.

My walk of faith started with The first Epistle of John, chapter 2:15-18.

My understanding of trust was found in the gospel of Jesus Christ Matthew 13:1-23.

These scriptures will change your mind, heart, and spirit and lead you closer to what God has and wants from you. I remember the first lie I told a young lady about where I had been, and I asked myself what the purpose was. She was still going to find out because GOD sees all. It started a debate in my head, and I would hear the devil say, at least she won't know. I then realized that we sometimes create a paradox in our thinking to fit our surroundings due to trying to fit in. You will find yourself going in unnecessary circles when you allow wrong to become correct. I only wanted to do what I deemed as right versus listening. We become so driven by our narrative that when given the instruction manual, we don't read it or open it due to our past teachings. It, in turn, creates the same generational cycle. I was a leader who wanted to follow the wrong instructions. I struggled to find my identity because I did not want to miss out or not be accepted by others. These same people barely acknowledged me. We change ourselves, put ourselves on hold, and stop doing what we can to change for the things we think matter. It is living with no standards as I was introduced into a world of repercussions and would find out the hard way. Each time I suffered the consequences of my actions, I would continue to do wrong. We become our own worst enemies because we are afraid of being alone. I hope that it doesn't cost you everything.

I now believe that I should have taken my time and followed the advice from my mother, who always told me to focus on school and listen to God for guidance in life. We always used the wrong thought process when peer pressure was involved. We didn't like to be left out, so we tried whatever was being presented without utilizing our conscience. If it is good for us, why do we have to hide to do it? Reading the Bible taught me everything I needed to know about becoming a man. Because of this, I became a lousy decision-maker who refused to listen. The Bible was introduced to me, and God was always addressed as the white man Jesus, and that was used to enslave our minds. The key is always to divide each other, and once this happens, the dictatorship and manipulation start, and a generation of distrust is formed. You then become confused because you have no identity.

Regardless, you have to choose the path you follow wisely. I know that prayer keeps us living through all the things that have happened in my life, my children's lives, my grandchildren's lives, and yours. No rules or religion.

We should treat God's children respectfully and allow Him to deal with them accordingly.

The hardest part of commitment is seeing the atmosphere change from bad to good and sustaining the work ethic to reach a positive momentum.

The fear of one's success allows the phrase (what I want) to supersede the understanding of what is needed on your path.

When God allows thought to become the purpose, He will enable your goals to become action.

If God led you there, He has a purpose for you being there. You can't experience His deliverance while complaining. God is trying to get rid of what's holding you back. You have to

believe that promises and blessings
are contrary to your disbelief.

I'm not about love until I love myself.

The funny part about wanting something is that
you have to practice the need for it.

The worst part of change is not seeing it
happen. It's catching time pass and not making
it happen.

My eulogy to my father-in-law
Morris Glasper, my father-in-law, represents
greatness. He has accomplished what most
people will not in a lifetime. Morris could
survive in any situation and kept his family first.
He was an accomplished father, role model,
neighbor, and leader in his family. Morris used
all his God-given talents to always provide for
his family and others, even when it wasn't
appreciated. He kept God in his heart through
his process of going home to be with the Lord.
As time lay across the footsteps of heaven, we
shall always honor greatness because his love
was real.

We must understand "one brick at a time"
because all bricks begin as a foundation.

Your inability to process what's important is
what holds you back. All things start with the
relationship with oneself.

Call me what you want, but broken is a name
you will not call me.

You can't look for new things while searching in
the same old place.

You look at some people's marriages and
wonder why they are still together. They never
stopped fighting to understand what "I will" and
"I do" truly mean.

I pray for better. Sometimes the weight of your
life's timeline can give you a heavy heart, but
understanding that God is at work in you
is the key.

Your life is made up of the past and present.
You control the future.

What you push out is what you reciprocate.

Are you residing in society's world or Jesus' world? Do you read, or do you follow?

Wake up and know that God got you.

If you can't see the finish line, that's because this is a marathon, not a race. Stop speedballing. Never chase wealth. Only pursue God's grace and mercy.

Don't believe the hype; Jesus is honest. Ask Him a question, and he will soon answer.

Why do we utter words in the atmosphere but don't put forth the effort? Be successful through actions, not words.

Real talk. You want to be treated like you matter, but you act like you're from a planet without rules, systems, and mass confusion. Your actions should align with your thoughts.

While you're hoping success knocks, someone else is planning for it.

How you get it always matters because that's how you will spend it.

Why are you in the no zone? If you have no plan, no goals, and no purpose, then it's you, not them.

You can't handle the truth if you are not ready to change.

The worst thing to do is to give up. Things will change as God has already written your life story.

I learned that my biggest enemy is complaining. That's why I had to let it go and get a new friend called 'moving forward.'

What does your mindset look like? Are your challenges everyone else's fault, or must you make better decisions?

Faith Is the truest glue to all relationships. If applied correctly, it can last a lifetime.

Faith is the answer, not man. Put your faith in

God, Jesus, and the Holy Spirit.

I declare war on lust, racism, injustice, d
igital slavery, lack of identity,
and the unfaithful.

Stay prayed up for battle. Choose God.

You must find your identity before someone else
puts their perception of you on you.

Celebrate each new day that God gives you. Be
blessed and pity party free.

The world is a distraction. It's time for men to
wake up, trim our planet and finally commit to
faith, hope, and love.

The best thing about my life is that I have God,
Jesus, and the Holy Spirit. Prayers go up, and
blessings come down.

If God tells me something,
I must exercise my faith.

Blessings will be in abundance when you

believe in God's Kingdom.

Men, your ability to commit to accepting a new you will be a struggle. It is vital to your success. Embrace your future.

Your age does not equate to your level of manhood. It's the actions that solidify the title.

How do you measure your growth?

You are busy staying the same but mad that no one noticed your old material.

The hardest part of depression is not listening to your inner self.

If you are not convinced that life is meaningful, keep doing what you want and watch what you need disappear.

Why complain about the problem when you are part of the issue? No plan should equate to no complaints.

What's more important, your pride or her
heart? Only a man can answer this.

God explained to me that she is my rib because I
am missing the best part of me without her.

You don't have to like me, but my name is what
God intended for me.

You must feel great about having bills in your
name. It empowers your mind
to pay them.

Your story is not defined by how you put
someone else down but by how you pick them
up in their time of need.

Anyone can pull the trigger, but can you
purposely remove the boy or girl
from you?

God woke me up today to be great.

Feel free to tell people that you are no longer

available for foolishness.

The best things in life are free: Hope, Faith, Love, Commitment, and Success. Choose wisely.

What drives your passion? Is it fuel or purpose?

Don't act like a secret and think that everyone knows who you are.

If you look to the right and left and no one is there, always look above and know that God got you.

Welcome to a new day. You are already blessed. Believe it, and let your light shine.

Although my physical money is not long like it used to be, God allows me to stretch what I have to grow for what I need.

Stop complaining about what you don't do for free.

Look at how free you are, somewhere other

than where you should be.

If you're getting it, why are you still looking like everyone who is not?

No faith, no results.

Your thoughts should always be measured by action.

You are no exception to the rule. You become what you have faith in.

Why are you mad at your position in life if you continue to choose no commitment or faith?

It's a blessing to wake up in my right mind, loving myself to love others.

The only way to eliminate a habit is to define why it became a habit in the first place.

I always switched lanes to move forward and pace myself for the journey.

Never allow the fear of who you are to stop you
from becoming who you need to be.

Stop saying what you're not going to become.
If you display the same habits,
you will get the same results.

This life, for me, is a choice of changes that
contribute to positive outcomes in life.
Be grateful.

If you are wondering about your next move,
allow God to give you your first step.
God is love.

You can't see me because you're not on my level.
Love, lead and live.

Once the purpose is added to your life, the big
picture becomes clear.

I love getting high on hope, faith, and love.
These are the best drugs I have ever taken
in my life.

When you truly put it In God's hands, no one

can stop His promise.

God gave us all the tools to be successful.
Stop complaining.

Have a plan, so nothing doesn't become
your life.

When times are hard for those without faith,
there is peace in God's word.

If you have seen death, been a part of failure,
and still have peace of mind, know that
God has allowed it.

How are you walking around with a negative
mentality but wanting something positive to
happen in your life?

The best part of life is you can change directions
when you're focused. The worst part is having
no purpose and going in circles.

I enjoyed my past because God gave me a way
out when the devil said I was nobody. Nobody is
more incredible than Jesus.

Never think you are alone because
you have a friend in Jesus.

A man is built to lead. When he becomes a great
listener and applies what he has learned,
it's imperative to lead by example.

A man's greatest attribute is his word,
not his penis.

When you respect yourself, you don't
accept anything else.

A man leads a woman only when
he becomes his path.

Goals influence change.

I love telling myself that I will take anything but
failure. I must speak this into existence.

He that keeps careless ways in his life shall
perish. Put down the ego and pride,
and choose God.

The best thing about me is that I understand I'm

nothing without God, Jesus, the Holy Spirit, and,
most importantly, my faith.

The greatest love you can have is
love for yourself.

The vision always requires a road map that is
entrusted with faith. Success requires
hard work.

My mirror shows my image differently since I
changed the inside of me.

It's always a wonderful feeling to own up to
what you say.

Know that life is priceless.

It's not just what she looks like that I'm in love
with; it's what she thinks.

Change in one's action dictates
the evolution of one's path.

Your thoughts, goals, and purpose
must align.

I have worn a lot of hats. But the one I loved
the most was becoming a husband to my
best friend.

Understand the importance of
working on oneself.

You can never lose something you never had.
Only prepare for the things that you shall own.

Anything that you have to rush for is not
worth your mental time.

The best part about transformation is that it is
both an inward and outward process.

My net worth is based on how positive
I can keep my life.

What's evident is that you must worship. Do you
see my smile? God washed away my ignorance.

When we get tired of being victims in our own
life, we need to honor Jesus, God, and the Holy
Spirit. They're always available.

I love living in His word and loving
who He is. I am grateful to be His
servant and child.

No workout can strengthen your body better
than the words of our Father God, Lord and
Savior Jesus Christ, and the Holy Spirit.

Live with understanding and love,
for we are all one.

Life is not what they say but only what we pray
for. God, we trust you.

We have a million things going on around us,
but only one thing matters- God woke us up
this morning.

Although the world around us constantly
changes, God remains the same.
Be blessed and show your faith.

The best thing about life is when you discover
yourself being someone else, and being the old
version of yourself becomes obsolete.

Understand that for all things received,
something is required. Blessings require praise.

The best part of marriage is knowing what
you've been through and loving where you are
going.

The only thing I am comfortable with is serving
God, Jesus, and the Holy Spirit. Love being
the greatest.

You can't ask your faith to increase if you only
want to watch others praise God.

I love the shoes that some of the men in my
family wear. Being a husband is the best brand
you can wear.

Don't get mad when someone tells you the truth
about yourself. Admit the fault so you can be
released from the situation.

The best part about love is when you
reciprocate what you dish out.

You can't keep pondering your past while

looking for a bright future. Release the shackles.

A loss is never a loss when you plan a different perspective and try again.

A boy can only become a man when he truly commits to the purpose in his name.

A lie can never be true if there is no foundation to support it.

God is real. You should strive to stand on his foundation.

The definition of being a man has integrity, truth, and character. No exceptions. Value becoming one.

A simple choice of words can empower a straightforward course of action.

Why steal something if you can obtain it through exhibiting your work ethic?

The more you detour through life, the harder it becomes to be patient and go through it.

Don't hate successful people because you chose
to be average—actions over words. Being
average should never be
the new normal.

When faced with a difficult decision, always
listen to whom it affects. Ask yourself the
following questions: What is the purpose?
Why is it necessary? When will it take place?
Where does it place you on your journey in life
to achieve your goals?

Live life with a smile.

Remember that when you do something, if it
doesn't make sense, it will cost you dollars.

The best thing about a plan is the standards you
set to ascertain the goal.

My biggest fear became my most outstanding
achievement. I learned how to trust in myself
and others.

What is in your closet? God is in the cleaning
business, whether it is secrets, lies, or

deception. Allow him to come into your life and change those things.

You wanted an explanation for a question that you created. The answer is inside of what you see in the mirror.

If your life is impacted by the things on the outside of you, the inside of you has no structure. Build from the inside out and become the standard for your life.

Start imitating the reflection and evolve the image.

Whether it's crackers or steak and lobster, you are eating. Stop complaining about the taste.

You are what you eat. So many people are processed. Nothing is made from scratch, and you wonder why the taste is incomplete.

To some people, you are worthless, but to our Father God, you are essential, necessary, and needed.

My past asked my future what had changed.
My future replied I got rid of
the old you.

My Father God never wants me to fail.
He only wants me to discover the greatness
inside of me.

Patience is the power to succeed.

The power switch is never off when God
is the one that flicked the switch
in the first place.

It feels great when there is no fear in your life
because you understand that the blood of Jesus
covers you. No matter the situation,
you are covered.

Marriage is a business that never stops
giving to its investors.

The greatest invention was never made of
materials. It was you. Believe and achieve.

You are only as great as your commitment to your actions.

I am genuinely grateful for everything that has transpired in my life thus far. It is truly a blessing to listen, learn and lead. Nothing in this world is impossible as long as commitment, compassion, and consistency are the driving force behind your foundation on earth. God, Jesus, and the Holy Spirit are at the head of all things because, without the BIBLE, none of this is truly possible.

Acknowledgments

Thank you to My mothers for their insight on the Importance of Becoming a Man. Louise Evans, Ann Wilson, Terry Butler, and Cheryll Mathis.

Please subscribe to my YouTube channel.
Check out the content and reach out if you or
someone you know needs counseling.
I am here to help.

—*Micheal Evans*

www.youtube.com/@mikeevans286

www.ingramcontent.com/pod-product-compliance
Lightning Source LLC
LaVergne TN
LVHW011333080426
835513LV00006B/326